步行穿過森林

Walking through the Jungle

Illustrated by Debbie Harter

Chinese translation by Sylvia Denham

mantra duets

穿過森林步行，

Walking through the jungle,

步行穿過森林

Walking through the Jungle

Mantra Publishing
5 Alexandra Grove
London N12 8NU
http://www.mantrapublishing.com

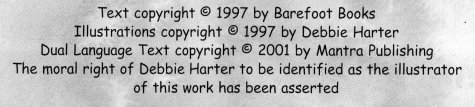

你見到什麼？

What do you see?

我想我看到一隻獅子
在我後面追我。

在海洋中浮游，

Floating on the ocean,

你見到什麼？

What do you see?

我想我看到一條鯨魚
在我後面追我。

在山嶺爬越，

Climbing in the mountains,

你見到什麼？

What do you see?

我想我看到一隻豺狼
在我後面追我。

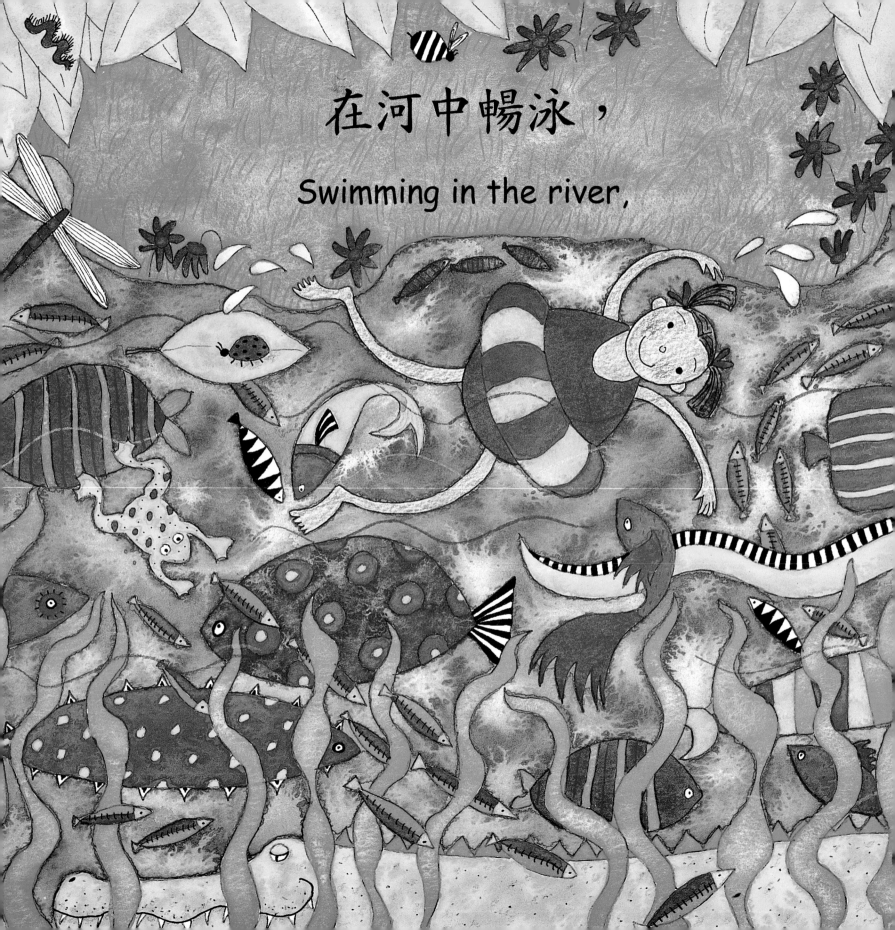

在河中暢泳，

Swimming in the river,

你見到什麼？

What do you see?

我想我看到一條鱷魚
在我後面追我。

在沙漠中跋涉遠足，

Trekking in the desert,

你見到什麼？

What do you see?

我想我看到一條蛇
在我後面追我。

在冰山上滑倒，

Slipping on the iceberg,

你見到什麼？

What do you see?

I think I see a polar bear, chasing after me.

Growl!

咆哮!

我想我看到一隻北極熊
在我後面追我。

奔跑回家吃晚飯，

Running home for supper,

你到過什麼地方？

Where have you been?

我走遍全世界才回來，

I've been around the world and back,

你猜我見過什麼。

And guess what I have seen.